pro bookmark™
for Bible Study

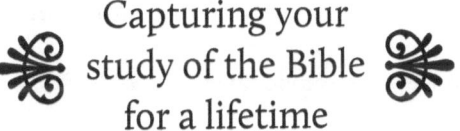

Capturing your study of the Bible for a lifetime

Dr. Roger D. Smith

ProBookmark for Bible Study:
Capturing your study of the Bible for a lifetime

© Copyright 2012 by Roger Smith. All rights reserved. No part of this book may be reproduced or transmitted in any form or by any means, electronic or mechanical, including photocopying, recording, or by any information storage and retrieval system, without written permission from the author. For information address Modelbenders Press, P.O. Box 781692, Orlando, Florida 32878.

Modelbenders Press books may be purchased for business and promotional use or for special sales. For information please contact the publisher.

PRINTED IN THE UNITED STATES OF AMERICA

Visit our web site at www.modelbenders.com

Designed by Adina Cucicov at Flamingo Designs
Cover image: © metsafile—Fotolia.com

The Library of Congress has cataloged the paperback edition as follows:

Smith, Roger
    ProBookmark for Bible Study: Capturing your study of the Bible for a lifetime.
    Roger Smith. – 1st ed.
    1. Christian Life—Inspirational   2. Bible Study Guides
    3. Motivational and Inspirational
    I. Roger Smith II. Title

ISBN 978-0-9843993-4-5

ProBookmark™ for Bible Study

THE TIME THAT YOU SPEND in personal Bible study is one of the richest experiences of your day. It is a journey into new ideas, new hopes, and new knowledge. Studying the Bible is the same as going on safari in Africa, touring Europe, or cruising the Mediterranean. It will show you new places, new people, and new ideas. You will gather knowledge and change your perspective on life. You always come away from Bible study changed in some way. Just as a trip to Africa will provide memories and experiences that you will never forget, the time spent in personal study will create indelible images and change the way you lead your life.

Because Bible study is so powerful and so important to your life, you should keep a record of your travels. Like carrying a camera or a journal on your tour through Europe, you should come away from study with pictures of what you have learned and notes on what you are going to do.

Most people rely on their memories to store everything they have ever read. They hope that their personal inspiration and insight from the Bible will remain with them for years. But, in practice, most of their ideas are quickly forgotten. Important information, inspiring stories, and life changing perspectives fade into the mists of an imperfect memory.

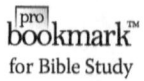
for Bible Study

ProBookmark™ for Bible Study is designed to change that. These simple pages will help you capture the important information from your personal Bible study. They become a photo album of your travels that you can save for as long as you live and be reminded of the most inspirational ideas you have ever experienced. Like a picture album, each phrase captured on a bookmark triggers a flood of memories, allowing you to relive them with the same richness you felt when you first studied the passages.

Don't let another Bible study pass through your hands and your mind without capturing its important ideas so they remain a part of your life forever. Use these bookmarks, save them, and review them to relive the rich treasure of ideas many times over throughout your life.

How to use ProBookmark™ for Bible Study

YOU CAN LOOK AT THESE bookmarks and understand instantly what you are supposed to do with them. The format is self-explanatory.

But here are some tips that will help you get the most out of these powerful tools.

1. **Start at the Beginning.** When you sit down for your Bible study, immediately fill out the top of one of these bookmarks. If you wait until you are halfway through, then half of the richness of your study will have been lost.

2. **Topic.** Your own Bible study may be by book or by topic. So this line could be either "Luke 6" or "Generosity".

3. **Date.** Be sure to fill in the date. You will be surprised at how many years a really good study will stick with you. It may seem that you read something just last year, when in fact more than five years have passed since you were changed by a particular study.

4. **Scripture List.** This is particularly helpful if you are doing a topical study. List all of the scriptures here so you can find them later and compare them to other studies. For a book

for Bible Study

study, list the specific chapters and verses that you covered in one study.

5. **Major Message.** In most cases you will not know what the major message is until you are well into it. This section is at the beginning of the bookmark because it is the summary that you will use later to recall what you have learned. Do not try to fill this in first, save it for later or last.

6. **Personal Impact.** There is a simple 5-star system to measure the impact that this study had on your mind, your heart, and your actions. Color in the number of stars that this study deserves for the knowledge, pleasure, or inspiration that it has given you.

7. **Inspiration.** When the study inspires you to think better thoughts or change your life, capture those ideas right away. Most study periods will provide several inspirations for your life.

8. **Action.** God has given us instructions for taking action in our own lives. Capture these here. This is the "To Do" list that you want to begin working on.

9. **Quotes.** The Bible has a knack for expressing ideas in words that are powerful and meaningful. Capture those verbatim in this section. You should also note the verse where these gems appear.

10. **Message Tracker.** As you read, keep track of the major points in the scriptures on the back side of the bookmark. This is a map of the story that runs throughout your study. The verses listed will guide you to really interesting ideas many years after they would have been lost in the paper folds.

11. **Many-to-One.** There is no reason that one study session must be summarized on just one bookmark. Feel free to use two or three bookmarks to capture the details of an exceptionally powerful study. These are your tools to use in a way that helps you the most.

12. **Improvements.** If you find a way to make these bookmarks more useful to you, please mark them up and let us know. We do not claim to have arrived at the perfect form yet. This bookmark comes from years of revisions. We would be thrilled to hear your ideas on how to make this tool better. Your suggestions could appear in next year's edition of *ProBookmark™ for Bible Study*.

Fruitful study and lifelong reminiscence lie ahead of you.

From now on, the treasures that emerge from every personal Bible study are going to be with you for the rest of your life.

Best Wishes,
Roger Smith
Luke 6:38

for Bible Study

topic.. date ....
scriptures studied..
....
major message..
....
.... personal impact ☆☆☆☆☆

inspiration ....
....
....
....
....
....

actions ....
....
....
....
....

quotes ....
....
....
....
....

verse — message tracker

topic .... date ....
scriptures studied ....
....
major message ....
....
.... personal impact ☆☆☆☆☆

inspiration ....

actions ....

quotes ....

verse message tracker

for Bible Study

topic .... date ....
scriptures studied ....
....
major message ....
....
.... personal impact ☆☆☆☆☆

💡 inspiration ....
....
....
....
....

actions ....
....
....
....
....

quotes ....
....
....
....
....

verse	message tracker

topic.. date ....

scriptures studied..

....

major message...

....

.... personal impact ☆☆☆☆☆

inspiration ....

actions ....

quotes ....

verse	message tracker

topic .... date ....
scriptures studied ....
....
major message ....
....
.... personal impact ☆☆☆☆☆

inspiration ....
....
....
....
....

actions ....
....
....
....
....

quotes ....
....
....
....
....

verse	message tracker

topic .... date ....

scriptures studied ....
....

major message ....
....
.... personal impact ☆☆☆☆☆

inspiration ....
....
....
....
....

actions ....
....
....
....
....

quotes ....
....
....
....
....

verse · message tracker

for Bible Study

topic... date ....
scriptures studied ....
....
major message...
....
.... personal impact ☆☆☆☆☆

inspiration ....

actions ....

quotes ....

verse | message tracker

topic .... date ....
scriptures studied ....
....
major message ....
....
.... personal impact ☆☆☆☆☆

💡 inspiration ....
....
....
....
....

❗ actions ....
....
....
....
....

❝ quotes ....
....
....
....
....

verse　　　　　　　　　　　　　　　　　　message tracker

topic .... date ....

scriptures studied ....

....

major message ....

....

.... personal impact ☆☆☆☆☆

💡 inspiration ....

....

....

....

....

❗ actions ....

....

....

....

....

❝ quotes ....

....

....

....

....

verse	message tracker

topic.. date ....

scriptures studied..
....

major message...
....
.... personal impact ☆☆☆☆☆

💡 inspiration ....
....
....
....
....
....

actions ....
....
....
....
....

quotes ....
....
....
....
....

verse   message tracker

for Bible Study

topic .... date ....
scriptures studied ....
....
major message ....
....
.... personal impact ☆☆☆☆☆

💡 inspiration ....
....
....
....
....

❗ actions ....
....
....
....
....

❝ quotes ....
....
....
....
....

verse	message tracker

topic .... date ....

scriptures studied ....
....

major message ....
....
.... personal impact ☆☆☆☆☆

💡 inspiration ....
....
....
....
....

❗ actions ....
....
....
....
....

❝ quotes ....
....
....
....
....

verse	message tracker

for Bible Study

topic.. date ....
scriptures studied ....
....
major message..
....
.... personal impact ☆☆☆☆☆

inspiration ....
....
....
....
....

actions ....
....
....
....
....

quotes ....
....
....
....
....

verse	message tracker

topic .... date ....

scriptures studied ....

....

major message ....

....

.... personal impact ☆☆☆☆☆

inspiration ....

....

....

....

....

actions ....

....

....

....

....

quotes ....

....

....

....

....

verse   message tracker

topic... date ....

scriptures studied..
....

major message...
....
.... personal impact ☆☆☆☆☆

inspiration ....
....
....
....
....

actions ....
....
....
....

quotes ....
....
....
....
....

verse	message tracker

topic... date ....
scriptures studied..
....
major message..
....
.... personal impact ☆☆☆☆☆

💡 inspiration ....
....
....
....
....
....

actions ....
....
....
....
....
....

quotes ....
....
....
....
....

verse   message tracker

topic .... date ....

scriptures studied ....

....

major message ....

....

.... personal impact ☆☆☆☆☆

inspiration ....

....

....

....

....

actions ....

....

....

....

....

quotes ....

....

....

....

....

verse   message tracker

topic.. date ....

scriptures studied...

....

major message...

....

.... personal impact ☆☆☆☆☆

inspiration ....

....

....

....

....

actions ....

....

....

....

quotes ....

....

....

....

verse | message tracker

topic... date ....

scriptures studied..

....

major message..

....

.... personal impact ☆☆☆☆☆

inspiration ....

....

....

....

....

actions ....

....

....

....

....

quotes ....

....

....

....

....

verse | message tracker

for Bible Study

topic .... date ....

scriptures studied ....

....

major message ....

....

.... personal impact ☆☆☆☆☆

inspiration ....

....

....

....

....

actions ....

....

....

....

....

quotes ....

....

....

....

....

verse

message tracker

for Bible Study

topic .... date ....
scriptures studied ....
....
major message ....
....
.... personal impact ☆☆☆☆☆

💡 inspiration ....
....
....
....
....
....

❗ actions ....
....
....
....
....
....

❝ quotes ....
....
....
....
....

verse   message tracker

pro bookmark™ for Bible Study

topic .... date ....
scriptures studied ....
....
major message ....
....
.... personal impact ☆☆☆☆☆

inspiration ....
....
....
....
....

actions ....
....
....
....
....

quotes ....
....
....
....
....

verse	message tracker

topic .... date ....
scriptures studied ....
....
major message ....
....
.... personal impact ☆☆☆☆☆

inspiration ....
....
....
....
....

actions ....
....
....
....
....

quotes ....
....
....
....
....

verse	message tracker

topic .... date ....

scriptures studied ....

....

major message ....

....

.... personal impact ☆☆☆☆☆

inspiration ....

....

....

....

....

actions ....

....

....

....

....

quotes ....

....

....

....

....

verse | message tracker

for Bible Study

topic.. date ....

scriptures studied ....

....

major message...

....

.... personal impact ☆☆☆☆☆

inspiration ....

....

....

....

....

actions ....

....

....

....

....

quotes ....

....

....

....

....

verse   message tracker

topic .... date ....
scriptures studied ....
....
major message ....
....
.... personal impact ☆☆☆☆☆

inspiration ....
....
....
....
....

actions ....
....
....
....
....

quotes ....
....
....
....
....

verse	message tracker

for Bible Study

topic... date ....
scriptures studied..
....
major message...
....
.... personal impact ☆☆☆☆☆

💡 inspiration ....
....
....
....
....

actions ....
....
....
....
....

quotes ....
....
....
....
....

verse

message tracker

for Bible Study

topic.. date ....
scriptures studied..
....
major message..
....
.... personal impact ☆☆☆☆☆

inspiration ....
....
....
....
....

actions ....
....
....
....
....

quotes ....
....
....
....
....

verse   message tracker

topic .... date ....

scriptures studied ....

....

major message ....

....

.... personal impact ☆☆☆☆☆

inspiration ....

....

....

....

....

actions ....

....

....

....

....

quotes ....

....

....

....

....

verse　　　　　　　　　　　　　　　message tracker

for Bible Study

topic.. date ....
scriptures studied...
....
major message..
....
.... personal impact ☆☆☆☆☆

💡 inspiration ....
....
....
....
....
....

❗ actions ....
....
....
....
....

❝ quotes ....
....
....
....
....

verse — message tracker

for Bible Study

topic.. date ....
scriptures studied..
....
major message...
....
.... personal impact ☆☆☆☆☆

inspiration ....

actions ....

quotes ....

61

verse   message tracker

topic .... date ....

scriptures studied ....

....

major message ....

....

.... personal impact ☆☆☆☆☆

inspiration ....

....

....

....

....

actions ....

....

....

....

....

quotes ....

....

....

....

....

verse / message tracker

topic.. date ....

scriptures studied...

....

major message...

....

.... personal impact ☆☆☆☆☆

inspiration ....

....

....

....

....

actions ....

....

....

....

....

quotes ....

....

....

....

....

verse   message tracker

for Bible Study

topic .... date ....
scriptures studied ....
....
major message ....
....
.... personal impact ☆☆☆☆☆

inspiration ....
....
....
....
....

actions ....
....
....
....
....

quotes ....
....
....
....
....

verse

message tracker

topic .... date ....
scriptures studied ....
....
major message ....
....
.... personal impact ☆☆☆☆☆

inspiration ....

actions ....

quotes ....

69

verse | message tracker

for Bible Study

topic .... date ....
scriptures studied ....
....
major message ....
....
.... personal impact ☆☆☆☆☆

💡 inspiration ....
....
....
....
....

❗ actions ....
....
....
....
....

❝ quotes ....
....
....
....
....

verse

message tracker

topic... date ....
scriptures studied..
....
major message..
....
.... personal impact ☆☆☆☆☆

inspiration ....
....
....
....
....

actions ....
....
....
....
....

quotes ....
....
....
....
....

verse

message tracker

topic.. date ....
scriptures studied...
....
major message..
....
.... personal impact ☆☆☆☆☆

💡 inspiration ....

✏️ actions ....

❝ quotes ....

verse message tracker

topic .... date ....

scriptures studied ....

....

major message ....

....

.... personal impact ☆☆☆☆☆

💡 inspiration ....

....

....

....

....

❗ actions ....

....

....

....

....

❝ quotes ....

....

....

....

....

verse	message tracker

pro bookmark™ for Bible Study

topic .... date ....
scriptures studied ....
....
major message ....
....
.... personal impact ☆☆☆☆☆

💡 inspiration ....
....
....
....
....

↘ actions ....
....
....
....
....

💬 quotes ....
....
....
....
....

verse	message tracker

bookmark for Bible Study

topic .... date ....

scriptures studied ....

....

major message ....

....

.... personal impact ☆☆☆☆☆

💡 inspiration ....

....

....

....

....

❗ actions ....

....

....

....

....

💬 quotes ....

....

....

....

....

verse | message tracker

topic .... date ....

scriptures studied ....
....

major message ....
....
.... personal impact ☆☆☆☆☆

💡 inspiration ....
....
....
....
....

❗ actions ....
....
....
....
....

❝ quotes ....
....
....
....
....

verse	message tracker

for Bible Study

topic.. date ....
scriptures studied...
....
major message..
....
.... personal impact ☆☆☆☆☆

inspiration ....

actions ....

quotes ....

verse	message tracker

topic... date ....

scriptures studied...

....

major message...

....

.... personal impact ☆☆☆☆☆

inspiration ....

....

....

....

....

actions ....

....

....

....

....

quotes ....

....

....

....

....

verse	message tracker

topic .... date ....

scriptures studied ....

....

major message ....

....

.... personal impact ☆☆☆☆☆

inspiration ....

....

....

....

....

actions ....

....

....

....

quotes ....

....

....

....

....

verse

message tracker

topic.. date ....

scriptures studied..

....

major message..

....

.... personal impact ☆☆☆☆☆

inspiration ....

....

....

....

....

actions ....

....

....

....

....

quotes ....

....

....

....

....

verse	message tracker

topic.. date ....
scriptures studied..
....
major message..
....
.... personal impact ☆☆☆☆☆

inspiration ....
....
....
....
....

actions ....
....
....
....
....

quotes ....
....
....
....
....

verse | message tracker

for Bible Study

topic.. date ....

scriptures studied..

major message..

.... personal impact ☆☆☆☆☆

inspiration ....

actions ....

quotes ....

verse | message tracker

for Bible Study

topic .... date ....
scriptures studied ....
....
major message ....
....
.... personal impact ☆☆☆☆☆

inspiration ....
....
....
....
....

actions ....
....
....
....
....

quotes ....
....
....
....
....

verse	message tracker
....	....
....	....
....	....
....	....
....	....
....	....
....	....
....	....
....	....
....	....
....	....
....	....
....	....
....	....
....	....
....	....
....	....
....	....
....	....
....	....
....	....
....	....
....	....
....	....
....	....
....	....
....	....
....	....

topic .... date ....
scriptures studied ....
....
major message ....
....
.... personal impact ☆☆☆☆☆

inspiration ....
....
....
....
....

actions ....
....
....
....
....

quotes ....
....
....
....
....

verse	message tracker

www.ingramcontent.com/pod-product-compliance
Lightning Source LLC
Chambersburg PA
CBHW031257290426
44109CB00012B/625